from BATTLEFIEL]

FRODSHAM AUXILIARY MILITARY HOSPITAL
1915 - 1919

by

Arthur R Smith

*A Short History - containing a remarkable
collection of previously-unpublished photographs*

FROM BATTLEFIELD TO BLIGHTY
- FRODSHAM AUXILIARY MILITARY HOSPITAL
1915 - 1919
by
Arthur R Smith

ISBN 1 902964 16 0

Editing, Typeset and cover design by William David Roberts MA
Avid Publications. © 2001

Front cover: Recruiting Poster for Voluntary Aid Detachments. Reproduced courtesy Imperial War Museum, London.
Frontispiece & rear cover: Nurses and patients at Frodsham Auxiliary Military Hospital. Circa 1916.

Other Publications from Avid are listed at the rear of this book.
To Order Books or Videos Direct Contact:-
Avid Publications, Garth Boulevard, Hr. Bebington,
Wirral, Merseyside, UK. CH63 5LS.
Tel / Fax (44) 0151 645 2047
Look at the books and videos via the internet on
http://www.avidpublications.co.uk
E-mail info@AvidPublications.co.uk

FOREWORD

It is a matter of some surprise that in the various historical accounts of bygone Frodsham, slight reference is made to the Frodsham Auxiliary Military Hospital which was established on Overton Hill in 1915. Indeed, it is difficult to think of any event in the town's long history which is more worthy of note. Between 1915 and 1919 over 3,400 wounded servicemen from all over the Empire were nursed back to health with the help of many local people, who also offered friendship and provided the soldiers with opportunities for leisure and entertainment.

For some years Arthur Smith has been adding to our knowledge of the local historical scene with his publications dealing with various aspects of Frodsham's past.

His latest research throws light on a proud and honourable but little known period in the history of the town.

In order to illustrate his book the author has used many recently-discovered unique and striking photographs. As usual he has explored in depth to present his investigation in some detail. This book is an influential memoir because it is the first to chronicle important events which were fading in the public memory.

We are indebted to Arthur Smith for this work which will give much satisfaction to all those who are interested in the history of our area.

H F Starkey 2001

The main hall of the hospital at Christmas 1916.

Acknowledgements

My thanks are due to the many people who have kindly supplied me with information for this history over quite a long period.

Top of the list come Tony and Mona Harding who allowed me to use the late Dorothea Urmson's collection of photographs and for their invaluable help in many other ways.

Secondly, I wish to thank Joan Taylor for all her special help and encouragement.

Next I am much indebted to the following people who have given me various details about the hospital: John & Margaret Adams, Edgar Brereton, Margaret Blythe, Eric Ellison, Rowland & Janice Edmonds, Les Finnerty, Jean Forster, Mary Gold, Rhoda Haughton, Kate Hill, Christine and Brian Lloyd, Tom Nicholls, David Nield, Dilys O'Neill, Walter Ormsby, Bernard Price, John & Sheila Scully, Judith Shore, Mrs Willis(Helsby), Len Worrall and Lance Yates.

I owe a great debt of gratitude to Mr H F Starkey for his helpful advice and encouraging comments and to Stuart Crook for his unstinting assistance with copying the photographs and with the preparation of the text on the computer. Also I wish to record my sincere thanks to the staff of the public institutions who have responded to my letters and sent me valuable information.

In particular the staff of the Cheshire Record Office, the St John's Ambulance Association, the British Red Cross and the British Medical Association.

I hope this short history helps to put on record the devoted service of the volunteers and the professionals who organised and staffed the Frodsham Hospital and provided a haven for some of those who were wounded in the First World War.

Finally I would like to mention the late Trevor Smith who shared his wide knowledge of the hospital with me and told many anecdotes about the staff. It was his stories that gave me the initial inspiration to undertake this line of research.

Arthur R Smith 2001

CONTENTS

Introduction

This is an account of the auxiliary military hospital established in Frodsham, Cheshire, during the First World War. From March 1915 sick and wounded men from many different regiments were looked after at Bellemonte, Overton, which is situated on the slopes of Frodsham Hill. By the time the hospital finally closed its doors on 15 September 1919, 3435 patients had been treated there.

The Frodsham hospital was one of hundreds of such voluntary institutions set up in the early years of the Great War. In these days of a comprehensive National Health Service, it is difficult to imagine how much reliance was once placed on voluntary effort, without which the returning wounded would have fared very badly. Often the staff of these hospitals was drawn from Voluntary Aid Detachments established in the years immediately prior to 1914.

Despite these preparations, no one could have imagined the appalling scale of the casualties in the 1914 - 18 War which was beyond all previous experience. For example, in the South African War, after three years fighting 21,157 men were wounded, whereas during 1916 alone the total number of wounded arriving in this country totalled 523,153.

As more evidence has come to light and the story pieced together, three main features of the Frodsham hospital have become apparent. Firstly, the considerable scale of public support for the venture; secondly, the admirable efficiency and dedication of the managers, doctors and nursing staff, many of whom were volunteers; thirdly, the relative speed with which most of the patients were re-habilitated.

By 1918 the auxiliary hospital at Overton was one of the largest of its kind in the county. Only two others - the Haigh Lawn at Altrincham and the hospital at Bromborough had nearly as many beds. From all accounts Frodsham had become a spacious, well-equipped and efficient hospital. As far as the evidence allows us to judge, it was a proud chapter in Frodsham's history.

CHAPTER 1-THE FOUNDING OF THE HOSPITAL

Origins of the Project

By December 1914 rumours abounded that Frodsham was to have its own auxiliary military hospital. Many preparations went on behind the scenes until finally the hospital opened to patients on 4th March 1915 in a rather unusual location. It was decided that the single storey roller-skating rink at Overton, erected in 1912 on land behind the Bellemonte Hotel, could be easily converted to provide suitable accommodation for wounded soldiers.

The original idea to raise money for the conversion of the skating rink had been put forward shortly after the outbreak of war. The owner of the premises, Mrs Parker Hoose, had been approached and she had agreed to loan the building for this purpose. Interested townspeople formed a committee and between £600 and £700 was quickly subscribed. Local tradesmen loyally gave support and volunteered assistance towards equipping the room. But hopes were suddenly dashed when it was learnt that the government might require the use of these premises for other purposes. However, according to a report in the *Chester Chronicle* for January 23 1915, the committee were soon informed that the authorities had no plans to use the building and that the premises could be made into a temporary hospital. The report goes on to state that the following week the committee met several times to put the work in hand immediately and that Messrs Lea of Runcorn were instructed to fit heating apparatus. The writer concludes '*the work will now proceed apace, so that the building will be ready in about three weeks time........*'

The building did not need much conversion as it consisted of a large skating hall with a fine wooden floor which had been kept in a polished condition. In fact this sprung maple floor was regarded as ideal for hospital purposes.

A Viewing Day and the Official Opening

On March 3rd 1915 a Viewing Day was held, when members of the public were invited to look around the new hospital. Admission took the form of a gift in kind. About 1500 people came and it is estimated that gift parcels amounted to over £35-00, which would be worth many times more than that sum today. In the afternoon everyone gathered in the main hall and Mr J J Crosfield, who was a director of Crosfield's Soap Works at Warrington and Chairman of the Board of Management of the hospital, gave an introductory address. He thanked people for their generous response in the initial stage of the venture and appealed to the people of Frodsham for their continued support. He hoped it would be regarded as an opportunity to "do something for our soldiers who were doing so much for us." Mrs Thomas then declared the hospital officially open.

A view of the hospital taken from the rear of the Bellemonte Hotel, showing the ingenious construction of the roof with its five arches to give a large open floor space. The entrance hall can just be seen in the centre of the picture, with the Matron's residence on the extreme right.

Another view of the hospital - this time taken from Overton village. On the left is Pump Cottage and across the road is Hawthorne Cottage, both of which were demolished many years ago. Note the pathways on the hillside, up and down which the more able patients would have walked many times.

Military Hospitals in the U.K.

At the outbreak of the First World War hospital accommodation in the U.K. consisted of 7000 equipped beds of which 2000 were in use. By the time of the Armistice in November 1918 the number of beds had increased to over 364,000. This vast increase had been achieved in a variety of ways. Additions were made to existing military hospitals and new ones constructed; territorial force general hospitals were opened and enlarged; special war hospitals were established in asylums, poor law institutions and other public buildings; places were found for the wounded in civil hospitals and, finally, a large number of auxiliary hospitals opened. These latter institutions were established and equipped by voluntary aid organisations and private individuals. As a matter of fact Cheshire led the way in the provision of auxiliary hospitals. According to the Annual Report of the Cheshire Branch of the British Red Cross Society for 1919, there were 60 auxiliary hospitals in the county by the summer of 1915 and by the end of 1918 the figure had reached 85. As the following table shows most of these were organised by the British Red Cross:

British Red Cross Society	76
Order of St John	4
Civil Infirmaries	2
Joint Committee of Red Cross and St John	1
Independent	2

Frodsham was one of the independent institutions. Although it had this independent or private status, after 1916 all auxiliary hospitals which were in receipt of a War Office capitation grant came under the jurisdiction of the County Director. These 85 hospitals provided a grand total of 4533 beds. In proportion to its population, as mentioned earlier, Cheshire had a larger number of auxiliary hospitals and beds than any other county. The total number of patients treated in its hospitals under the jurisdiction of the County Director from October 1914 to the final demobilisation in 1919 amounted to 74,412 (exclusive of out-patients).

Mr T Stanley Bower

Before the opening of the Frodsham Military hospital the Board of Management had appointed Mr T Stanley Bower of Overton Hall, Five Crosses, Frodsham, as the Officer-in-Charge. In this role he was responsible for the administration, discipline and maintenance of the hospital, whereas it was the duty of the Matron to oversee the wards and the nursing staff. She was responsible to the Medical Officer for her patients.

Almost certainly Mr Bower relied on a small team of volunteers to serve as the administrative staff. In due course the Board received a War Office capitation allowance for every patient being treated at the hospital. In addition certain items, for example the uniforms worn by the patients, would be supplied by the War Office.

The Medical Officer

Shortly after the outbreak of war, Dr William Edward Burton volunteered for service with the RAMC. In March 1915 he was appointed as the Medical Officer at the Frodsham Hospital. Capt Burton had qualified LSA London 1889 and MRCS Eng 1891. In the summer of 1916 he was succeeded by Dr Ellison but he continued to help at the hospital whenever needed.

Capt Burton (fifth from the left in the back row) with nurses and patients.

Dr Harold Blades Ellison MA MB, who resided at "Brentwood," Red Lane, Frodsham, served as the Medical Officer until late in 1917. Dr Ellison, whose family lived in Hoylake, came to Frodsham in 1912 to join Dr Burton's practice.

Visiting Times

Visiting days were Wednesdays from 2pm to 4pm and Sundays from 4pm to 6pm. Opportunities to visit patients must have been in considerable demand as it was soon decided to regulate the numbers by means of permits. Permits

In the centre are the first Matron, Mrs Brown, and Dr Ellison, with Sister Davis on his left and two other Sisters behind him. The rest of the nurses would be volunteers. Mrs Brown served at the hospital from March 1915 until the summer of 1917.

could be obtained from Mr R H Dutton, the Honorary Treasurer, at Parr's Bank in Main Street, Frodsham. In the early summer of 1915 Mr Bower requested that local residents with motor cars and gardens consider placing them at the disposal of the wounded soldiers in the hospital from time to time.

Local people having their photograph taken with patients whom they have befriended.

CHAPTER 2 - THE HOSPITAL BUILDINGS

The Skating Rink

In late Victorian times there were two sets of attractions on Frodsham Hill - Mersey View Recreation Grounds and, the less well known, Bellemonte Pic-nic and Pleasure Grounds. In 1865 Robert Briscoe had opened the first tea-room at Mersey View. Slowly over the next thirty or forty years more attractions were added until by the end of the century not only had the tea-room been considerably enlarged but parents and children enjoyed the swing boats, the donkey rides and games on the green. Mersey View had become a Mecca for family and Sunday School outings.

In 1908 Mrs Parker-Hoose, who had inherited the Recreation Grounds, gave orders for the helter-skelter to be constructed. It soon proved to be worth every penny of the £300 which it cost to build as children from miles around enjoyed its thrilling slide. By the year 1912 roller-skating had become a fashionable pastime, and in the same enterprising vein, she opened the skating rink as a further attraction at the Bellemonte Pic-nic and Pleasure Grounds.

These grounds, about 6 acres in extent, were situated to the rear of the Bellemonte public house and consisted of a bowling green, a croquet lawn, a gymnasium, archery butts and a small dancing room - some of which can be seen marked on the map below.

A section of the 1910 Ordnance Survey Map for Frodsham showing the Bellemonte Hotel and the bowling green, with the gymnasium and dancing room on the land to the rear.

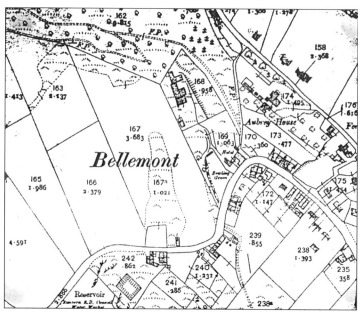

A beautifully drawn poster, probably dating from the early 1900s before the days of the skating rink, advertising the various attractions at the Bellemonte Picnic Grounds. Note the sub-titles at the bottom of each picture.

13

The roller-skating rink proved very popular, especially with parents and children. Older residents can remember many stories about the happy times their parents and grandparents enjoyed there. As stated earlier, Mrs Parker Hoose lent these premises early in 1915 when the urgent need for more military hospitals arose.

Gradual Expansion

When the hospital opened in March 1915 it had just 30 beds in the main hall but soon 20 more were added. Later, in the same year, a further 20 were brought into use filling the existing single room. This original area became known as Ward I.

Pressed by the military authorities to extend the accommodation, the Board decided to order the construction of a long wooden hut, which would provide room for an additional 50 beds. This building was completed in December 1915 - the cost being met through the generosity of local subscribers. By Christmas of that year there were 80 patients in the hospital.

By March 1917 there were 130 beds in the two wards, including six in a verandah for open-air treatment. At this point the managers arranged for a further 40 beds to be provided in tents. But, later in the year, it was decided that accommodation in tents was impractical and they were returned to the Army. Next the Board proposed to increase the verandah-type of accommodation to provide a further 26 to 30 beds. To accomplish this they gave instructions in August 1917 for another new building to be erected, a special feature being its glass-panelled doors, which could be opened wide to allow in plenty of fresh air and sunlight. Those concerned with the finances must have been relieved to hear that the cost of this new development would not fall on the Board of Managers as the money had been donated.

In this way the hospital was gradually enlarged until, as we have seen, it had accommodation for a total of 160 beds, although in 1918 the average number of in-patients resident daily was only 125.

Thus, in its final form, the hospital comprised a main ward, which could hold up to 70 beds, and two subsidiary wards - the wooden hut and the new building of August 1917 – an operating theatre, a dining area and kitchen, a recreation room and a number of stores. These three wards and the other rooms are shown in the plan on the next page.

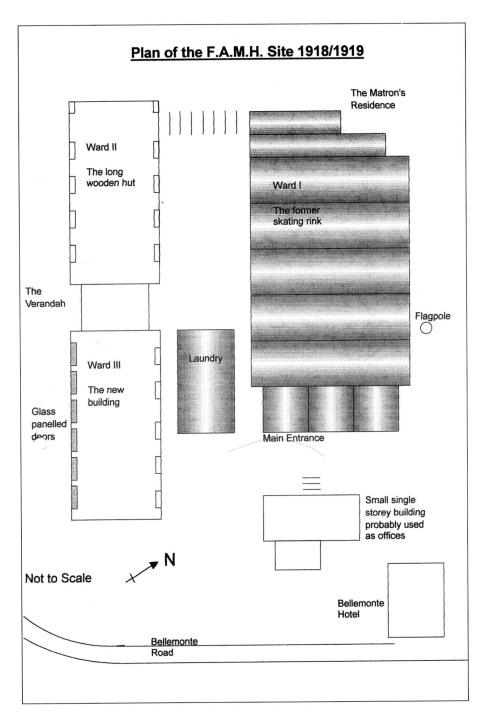

Plan of the F.A.M.H. Site 1918/1919

The Matron's Residence

Ward II

The long wooden hut

Ward I

The former skating rink

Flagpole

The Verandah

Laundry

Ward III

The new building

Glass panelled doors

Main Entrance

Small single storey building probably used as offices

N

Not to Scale

Bellemonte Hotel

Bellemonte Road

Plan of the F.A.M.H. Site 1917/1918

The main hall in 1915 showing how the beds had to be set out in double rows to accommodate the growing number of patients.

Early in 1916 extra accommodation was provided by the addition of a long wooden hut - known as Ward II. This building stood on the hillside behind the main hall.

On the left is the new building constructed in August 1917. The main part of the hospital (Ward I) can be seen between the two white buildings.

Another view of the new building clearly showing the glass-panelled doors opened wide to allow in plenty of fresh air and light.
The entrance to Ward I can be seen on the extreme right.

The so-called balcony or verandah between Ward II and Ward III in January 1919. The patients from left to right are: Pte Lewis, Cpl Spencer, Pte Cockcroft and Pte Wilson. These four men slept in this room. Sister Davis is holding the dog, whilst Nurse Urmson stands to the right of Pte Wilson. Note Nurse Urmson's efficiency stripe on her right sleeve. These stripes were awarded for long service and experience.

Two of the patients in front of the main entrance to Ward I.

The Bellemonte Hotel as it appears today in the year 2001.It was built in 1872 by James Rigby who sold it in 1897 to Mrs Parker Hoose. Its licensee at the time of the military hospital was Wilfred Sampson.

As the photographs show the new building proved to be a big improvement on Ward II. The large glass-panelled doors could be opened wide in the summer time making it easy for beds to be brought out on to the field. The hospital authorities commented that the advantages of this would be to make better use of the spare beds. At the same time the severe cases would benefit enormously by the open-air treatment. With this additional space the total number of beds had now reached 160. Eventually more beds were added in existing wards until by 1918 the total number had reached 190 – making Frodsham one of the largest auxiliary hospitals in the county.

CHAPTER 3 - THE MEDICAL AND NURSING STAFF

Dr Ellison MA MB

According to the Medical Register, Dr Ellison qualified MRCS LRCP in 1908 and MB BCh. in 1910 (Camb and Liverpool). Later that year he became the Gynaecological House Surgeon and House Physician at the Royal Infirmary, Liverpool. As mentioned earlier, he moved to Frodsham in 1912 to work with Dr Burton as a family doctor. During 1915 he assisted at the newly established hospital at Overton, but early in the New Year he volunteered for service in the RAMC and was posted to a field station in Northern France. After many months of intensive medical and surgical work behind the front line, he was sent back to England. In the summer of 1916 he took up an appointment as the Medical Officer at the Frodsham hospital. During the next few months he worked extremely hard to cope with the increasing number of casualties who were being sent to Overton.

Dr Ellison and the first Matron, Mrs. Brown, sitting in deck chairs, pose for a photograph with some of the nurses and soldiers. A picture taken in the early days of the hospital before uniforms were issued to all patients.

Dr Ellison resigned his position in August 1917 when he received his recall to the RAMC. He was succeeded as the Medical Officer by Dr Adams. After the war Dr Ellison resumed his work as a general practitioner. During the many years that he served as a doctor in Frodsham he was noted for his good humour and his generosity towards his less well-off patients. Often he would ignore the matter of payment for his services.

He lived at "Brentwood," Red Lane, and later at "Thornhill," Fluin Lane, Frodsham. In retirement he moved to 9A Park Road, West Kirby, Wirral. He died in 1959 aged 79.

Dr Alfred Adams

Starting his medical career later than most, Dr Adams qualified M.B., Ch.B., with honours at Liverpool University in 1910. Two years later he took his M.D. and the Diploma in Public Health. He held the Johnston Colonial Fellowship in Pathology and Bacteriology at Liverpool for a year before being appointed the Medical Superintendent of the Liverpool Sanatorium, Delamere Forest, in 1912. He remained in this post, except for a break during his military service, until he retired in 1938. Dr Adams was in many ways a pioneer in the early institutional treatment of pulmonary tuberculosis, and conducted the difficult work of the sanatorium with great skill and initiative.

In the First World War he served in the RAMC, with the rank of captain, in France, Gallipoli and Salonika and, in the latter, he was in charge of the No 2 Mobile Bacteriological Laboratory. After this service abroad, probably through injury or ill-health, he returned to England. It was at this point that he became the Medical Officer at the Frodsham auxiliary hospital.

When the hospital closed in September 1919 he resumed his full time post at the Liverpool Sanatorium. In the latter part of his life Dr Adams lived at 15 Woodvale Road, Knutsford, where he died, after a short illness, in January 1943.

Dr Selby MBE

Dr Thomas James Selby. who for many years had a surgery at the Rock, Main Street (now High Street)) Frodsham, also served as a Medical Officer at the auxiliary hospital. He had gained his MB at the University of Durham in 1892 and his LRCP and LRCS at Edinburgh. After the war he became the Medical Officer of the National Children's Home at Newton Hall and held a similar position at the Poor Law Hospital of the Runcorn Union. At a later date he was awarded the MBE. He retired to the Lake District and lived at Wordsworth House, Cockermouth.

The Nurses

The number of nurses serving at the hospital gradually increased until by 1918 there were twenty three, including the Matron. As one would expect there was an acute shortage of nurses in all types of hospitals during the First World

War. With the dreadful carnage on the Western Front and thousands of casualties returning home there was soon a desperate need for more hospitals and more nurses. Many volunteers were recruited. They were known as VADs - the Voluntary Aid Detachment nurses. After a very short training they were thrown in to the hard and difficult work of tending the sick and wounded. Often frowned upon by the trained nurses, unpaid and overworked, they were among the true heroines of the war. As far as we know most of the ordinary nurses at the Frodsham hospital were VADS.

Mr. Stanley Bower with the doctors and nursing staff of the hospital in 1918. Seated in the second row from the front, left to right, are Dr Adams, Mr. Bower, the Matron and Dr Selby. In the third row from the front (L to R) are two nurses, then Sister Mather, Sister Davis and two other Sisters.

Voluntary Aid Detachments

In the years immediately before the outbreak of war, Voluntary Aid Detachments were established in many towns and villages under the auspices of the Red Cross and the St John's Ambulance Association. Shortly after the opening of hostilities the War Office recommended that these Detachments should be utilised for service with the RAMC. Members of these VADs were to serve in military hospitals when RAMC personnel were called to the front. In other places they were called upon to staff the auxiliary hospitals. A good example of this type of arrangement was the Red Cross Hospital established at Helsby, Cheshire, in 1915. The hospital was set up at the Britannia Recreation Hall and staffed by the No 72 Helsby Women's Detachment, with Mrs. Eva

Horner serving as the Commandant. Orderlies and transport services were provided by the No 13 Men's Detachment - Commandant: Mr. F S Horner. Mr. and Mrs. Horner lived at Gorsefield, Helsby.

As will be seen from the figures given below, the Red Cross played a considerable part in nursing the wounded. In the first year of the war the volunteer nurses, cooks, kitchen maids, clerks, ward maids, laundresses and motor drivers, who staffed the hospitals in Cheshire, came from 78 Red Cross Voluntary Aid Detachments (65 Women's and 13 Men's) with a personnel of some 2300. By the end of 1918 the total number of Voluntary Aid Detachments working in the County had reached 113 (97 Red Cross and 16 St John). Of these 89 were Women's and 19 Men's Detachments - five being Transport Units, for which both men and women were eligible. The total number of War Office brassards (badges) issued to members of mobilised V.A.D.s totalled 5918 and the estimated number of personnel directly employed in connection with the sick and wounded about 8000. Rather remarkably, the Overton hospital did not fit exactly into this pattern because it was organised independently and there was no Voluntary Aid Detachment in Frodsham for it to draw upon.

The nearest St John's Voluntary Aid Detachments were at Winsford and Chester and the nearest Red Cross units at Helsby, Chester, Northwich and Warrington. VAD nurses were expected to hold current first aid and home nursing certificates. Each course took six weeks and, almost certainly, the nurses at Overton would have been trained by the Red Cross or the St John's Ambulance Association through one of the neighbouring detachments mentioned above or they would have served a probationary period in a local hospital. It should be remembered that none of the VAD nurses in any district were paid or given a uniform allowance, except in special circumstances. (See Appendix III for how VADs units were established in Kent before the war and then used to staff the newly organised auxiliary hospitals in that county).

Although it had an independent status, the F.A.M.H. came under the general jurisdiction of the War Office. For this purpose initially it was affiliated to the 1st Western General Hospital, Liverpool, but later transferred to the War Hospital, Cheshire.

Miss Winifred Davies

The actual credentials of only one VAD nurse at Overton have come to light. The late Mrs. Freda Bailey, nee Miss Winifred Davies, was enrolled as a Special Probationer of the St John's Detachment 1130 of West Lancs on the 6th of November 1918 as shown in the certificate overleaf. As far as we know Miss Davies then served at the Overton hospital until its closure in October 1919. There are no grounds for believing that any Queen Alexandra Nurses - the corps of specialist nurses set up for the Army - ever served at the hospital.

However the Matron and the four or more Sisters who were employed would be trained nurses. This small staff of professional nurses were assisted by the numerous volunteers.

Miss Davies's Certificate of Enrolment in the West Lancs Voluntary Aid Detachment.

St John's Ambulance Brigade

Members of the St John's Ambulance Brigade worked as orderlies and stretcher-bearers. They met the trains carrying the wounded at Chester Station and conveyed the men to the various hospitals. At their destination the Ambulance Corps did just whatever they were told to do to help the doctors and nurses give comfort to their patients. Usually this meant they undressed, bathed and fed the soldiers and, in other ways, attended to their needs.

The following extract from the *Chester Chronicle* for Saturday 18th August 1917 illustrates the work of the St John's Ambulance men:

"On Monday evening the inmates of the Auxiliary Military Hospital were increased by the arrival of 40 more wounded soldiers, all cot cases. The party consisted of men from various regiments, including four Canadians. The men had made a quick and comfortable journey from Northern France. They left Le Havre at 8am and arrived in Frodsham at 6-30pm and were bedded down by 7-30pm. Local cars left the Town Hall at 5pm accompanied by Messrs Powell, Clarke, Goodall, Patten and Jones of the local Ambulance Corps and under the charge of Commandant Bower."

According to another report in the *Chester Chronicle* in November 1917, classes were being held at the Frodsham Fire Station to increase the strength of the local Ambulance Corps. The report highlights the need for more trained personnel to deal with new arrivals at the Overton Hospital. The instructor at these classes was Dr Selby.

Members of the local St John's Ambulance Brigade with their wives and friends. Third from the right on the front row is Frederick William Booth, who contracted empiema whilst attending to patients at the hospital. Dr Selby, in the white coat, can be seen standing in the back row.

Dr Ellison and the Matron sitting on a bench in Ward I, Christmas 1916. Note the elaborate decorations, including the Christmas tree on the right.

Ward II - the long wooden hut - Christmas 1916. The highly polished state of the tables, chairs and the floor are very impressive and suggest that perhaps, at times, this was more of a convalescent hospital than one dealing with acute medical or surgical cases.

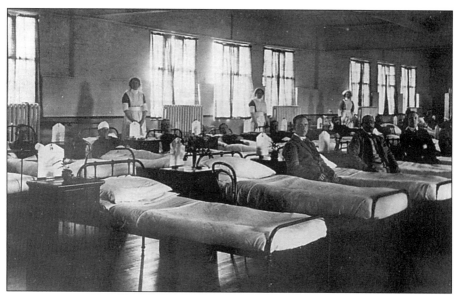

Bed patients and convalescents, with their nurses, pose for a photograph in Ward I.

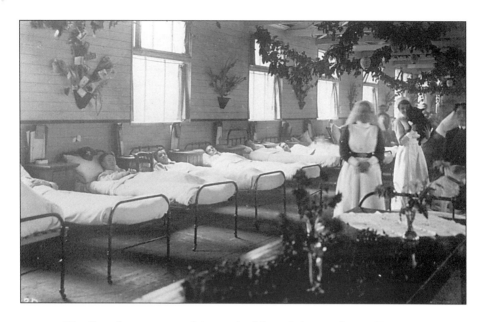

The first three patients lying in bed from left to right are Ptes Nutting, Leyland and Peacock. On the right are Sister Mather, Nurse Campbell and the Matron. Ward II - Christmas 1917.

Dr Adams and the new Matron, Miss B Stevens, at the main entrance to the hospital.

The Matron, with her two dogs, outside her residence at the northern end of the hospital.

Ward II - Christmas 1917. On the left is Sister Mather and behind her Nurse Urmson. Sitting at the table are the Matron and Nurse Cameron.

Christmas dinner, 1917. This is the only photograph which shows the main dining room. Note the billiard table in the foreground.

Sister Davis (centre) with the patients of Ward III at Christmas in 1918. Nurse De Silva is standing on the right.

*The same patients and nurses in a different grouping. Both this and the
previous photograph give a good view of the interior of Ward III.*

A Nurse's Life: Duties and Hardships

If the working conditions in other military hospitals in those days are
anything to go by, then almost certainly the nurses at Overton worked long
hours - maybe ten or twelve hours each day, probably starting at 7-00am or 7-
30am. Then every few weeks there would be night duty to face - a long stretch
from 8pm to 8am. All manner of unpleasant tasks had to be undertaken -
ranging from cleaning up serious wounds to supporting freshly amputated
limbs whilst they were dressed and dealing with badly suppurating infections.
Washing and bathing severely wounded patients would be no easy task, and
constantly emptying bed pans and similar chores were not the pleasantest of
jobs.

No doubt many of the nurses faced a long journey to and from their work
which may have entailed walking a considerable distance and certainly some
would have trekked from the bus stop in Frodsham Main Street or from the
railway station up the hill and back again every day. Pleasant enough in
summer, perhaps, but not so enjoyable on cold and wet winter mornings and
evenings. Conditions in the wards at Overton must have been unpleasant at
times, especially in the hutted accommodation, where the only heating was
provided by stoves. This must have left some parts of the rooms bitterly cold
in winter and, other parts, warm but maybe full of fumes. In hot weather these
wooden huts would become unbearably stuffy - no doubt this is the reason why
some of the photographs show patients lying in their beds in the open air.

"The Testament of Youth"

One of the few accounts of the life of a VAD nurse in the First World War is contained in Vera Brittain's book "The Testament of Youth." Unfortunately no such description by a Frodsham nurse has come to light, not even a few letters or an extract from a diary. But at least we have the evidence of the photographs. To help the reader imagine the probable background to some of these pictures, a few extracts from Vera Brittain's book are quoted below.

One could easily imagine that any one of the Frodsham nurses could have been in the following situation: *"When I began to work in the long hut, my duties consisted chiefly in preparing dressing-trays and supporting limbs - a task which the orderlies seldom undertook because they were so quickly upset by the butcher's-shop appearance of the uncovered wounds. Soon after I arrived I saw one of them, who was holding a basin, faint right on top of a patient." p. 211*

A more unexpected problem might well have arisen from the incessant playing of gramophone records in the wards. Probably many of the soldiers at Overton enjoyed listening to the popular songs of the day such as *"If I were the only girl in the world,"* or *"When Irish eyes are smilin'"* but, as Vera Brittain says, the constant repetition of these songs may have been a source of considerable irritation to the nurses.

In the next extract Vera Brittain describes how she felt about the preparations for Christmas at her military hospital in Camberwell. No doubt the Frodsham nurses had similar experiences. *"The night before Christmas Eve I found my ward transformed into the gay semblance of a sixpenny bazaar with Union Jacks, paper streamers, crinkled tissue lampshades and Christmas texts and greetings, all carried out in staggering shades of orange and vivid scarlet and brilliant green. In the cheerful construction of red paper bags, which I filled with crackers and sweets for the men's Christmas stockings, I found that the hours passed quickly enough." p. 234.*

Judging by the photographs of the wards at Christmas, the nurses and other helpers must have spent considerable time making dozens of streamers and garlands, and in decorating the walls with foliage. Also, no doubt, the Frodsham nurses filled brightly coloured paper bags with "crackers and sweets" for the men's Christmas stockings, and then felt a warm glow of benevolence when their patients woke early on Christmas morning and reached for their home-made presents.

Looking Behind-the-Scenes

Although the photographs constitute an almost unique visual record of life in an auxiliary hospital, they do inevitably present a somewhat sanitised view of what went on there. They are snapshots taken of the happier moments, for example, of patients and nurses in neat and tidy wards at Christmas time or outside on the field on a warm summer's day. Unfortunately the photographs do not depict any of the less pleasant side of hospital life. In the whole collection of 150 photographs there is no record (nor would one expect there to be in those times) of the nurses at work dressing serious wounds, or emptying bedpans, changing sheets or scrubbing bed mackintoshes; lifting patients, washing and bathing them, and all the other countless tasks that they had to undertake in the course of a day's work.

Similarly there is no record of the behind-the-scenes work of the cooks and kitchen staff preparing hundreds of meals every day and of the rest of the innumerable jobs that were essential to keeping everybody well fed. For example, the planning of the meals, buying the foodstuffs, the checking and carrying in the deliveries, the cooking and serving of the food, and then, afterwards, the piles of plates, dishes and cutlery which had to be washed. Another big undertaking for the staff was the cleaning of the wards and the constant changing of the bed linen. There is one photograph which shows a mound of sheets ready for the laundry but with 190 beds what a busy place that department must have been. And how on earth did they cope with all that drying - not to mention the ironing!

Then there was the general caretaking: keeping the boilers going for the radiator heating and supplying coal or coke for the stoves. Also the daily routine of sweeping the floors, dusting and polishing the furniture.

When a convoy arrived with thirty or forty new casualties there were extra demands made on everyone's energies. The patients, some probably suffering terrible injuries, had to be carefully washed and bathed, then dressings administered and hospital uniforms supplied. One should not forget one important fact lying behind all this - that the majority of the nurses were volunteers who gained very little financial reward for their labours.

A Sad Time

Undoubtedly one of the worst events that the nurses and doctors faced was the death of a patient. Such occasions were rare at the Overton hospital, but a few deaths did occur as we shall see in a later chapter. The first patient to die there was a Pte Alfred Carter and his funeral is described in some detail in the *Chester Chronicle* of Saturday 25th December 1915:

"Pte Carter of the 1st Leicestershire Regiment who died at the Frodsham military hospital on Thursday last, was interred in the Overton churchyard with military honours on Tuesday."

The report goes on to explain that Pte Carter had been at the front for 14 months, but fell sick. He had been brought to the hospital three weeks before but it had been necessary to perform an operation on him. Exactly why he died subsequently is not disclosed. The report continues: *"The procession from the hospital to the churchyard was led by a firing party composed of men from the Royal Field Artillery under Corporal Mallard. The coffin, which was covered with a Union Jack, was wheeled on a bier. The bearers were all patients at the hospital and were in the charge of Sgt Davies, formerly police constable at Kingsley, who had been wounded in the face, body and leg. The other bearers were Corporal Keife, Corporal Henderson, Ptes Smith, Lefevre, Newsham, Barton, Massey and Newbury. The coffin was followed by the sister of the deceased and several members of the hospital staff, including Mrs. Brown (matron), Sisters Speak, Fraser, Green and Gaskell. In the procession were also Capt Burton - the medical officer of the hospital, Mr. Bower - superintendent, Dr Ellison and the following patients: Ptes Manning, Rutter, Dobson, Robinson, Barton, Ravenshill, Diball, M Wood and L/Corporal James. At the entrance to the church and in the street a large number of people had assembled and many followed the cortege into the church. It was the first military funeral from the hospital and it cast a gloom over the village of Overton. In the church and at the graveside, Reverend Myres officiated. After the service three volleys were fired over the grave and the 'Last Post' sounded."*

This poster was used to recruit VAD nurses for overseas service in 1915.
(Courtesy Imperial War Museum)

Sister Davis (at the front), Sister Mather, Nurse Williamson and Miss Melhuish make use of a workman's ladder to pose for a photograph, with the framework of the new Ward III clearly visible in the background. August 1917.

Nurse De Silva (on the right) is wearing an armband of the St John's Ambulance Brigade.

Sisters and nurses enjoying a respite from their labours.

Sorting the laundry.

35

Some of the staff of Ward II in May 1918. From the rear, left to right, are Nurses De Silva, Urmson and Galloway, Sister Mather and Nurse Campbell.

Nurse Urmson with her colleagues from Ward II.

Nurses Guile, Willis, Williamson and Campbell at the rear, with Nurse De Silva seated in the foreground. In the background is the near side of Ward III - the new building.

Two patients equipped with walking sticks. Note the small white building behind them - the so called "balcony" between Wards II and III.

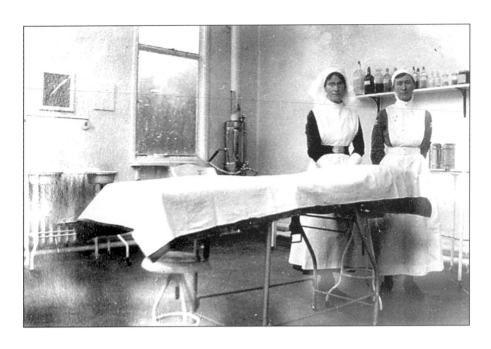

A Sister and one of the nurses stand ready for duty in the small operating theatre. Operations were carried out once a week usually on Tuesdays.

One of the orderlies pauses for a few moments on his rounds with the dressings trolley.

The Matron with "Hughie" outside the main entrance. "Hughie" was almost certainly the District Nurse.

Picnic time on the hill for some of the nursing staff. Nurses Hickson and De Silva are in the foreground, with Mr. Bower sitting on the left at the rear. Could that be Mrs. Parker Hoose standing at the back of the group?

CHAPTER 4 - PUBLIC SUPPORT
Donations and Fund-Raising Events

One of the most remarkable features of the story of the Frodsham Auxiliary Hospital is the high level of public support for the venture. As we have seen the original premises were made available by Mrs Parker Hoose. Gifts poured in on the first Viewing Day and the success of the whole enterprise was only made possible by generous public subscriptions. Many of the staff gave their services free. Most of the nurses were volunteers, the doctors often attended their patients free of charge and much of the administrative work was done without payment.

At the same time the hospital received a relatively large sum in the form of a War Office capitation allowance with which it was able to meet the various bills for provisions, equipment (for example new beds), medicines, drugs, surgical appliances, some salaries and wages, laundry and other miscellaneous expenses (see the Accounts to December 1916 - Appendix 1). By 1916 the rate of the capitation allowance had been raised to 3 shillings per patient per day. In addition to the public subscriptions, during the first six months of the hospital's existence donations in kind continued to arrive almost daily. Over twenty per cent of the patients' food and provisions were supplied through these gifts.

However, as the accounts demonstrate, over one third of the hospital's income came from subscriptions and donations of one form or another. A small but nonetheless significant part of this income came from individual or school fund- raising efforts. In June 1915 Miss Linaker and Mrs. N Linaker raised £14 - 00 by means of the Black Bag trick! Unfortunately for today's fund-raisers, no details are given of "the trick," but it is interesting to learn in same report how the managers spent this particular sum of money - on hot water bottles, cushions, dressing gowns, a chair and a collecting box.

On Wednesday 1st March 1916 pupils from "The Close" private school at Overton raised over £12 - 00 for the hospital with a performance of *"Scenes from Cranford."* The proceeds were used to provide five garden seats for use of the soldiers in the hospital grounds and six fancy tablecloths for the ward tables.

The Ryder Boys staged a similar fund-raising event with a Dramatic Performance at the Drill Hall in Main Street, Frodsham, at the end of October 1916. What a pity that we do not have any details of who these actors were or of what they performed! However the venture must have been well attended as it raised over £89 - 00. In a letter to the organisers, the Honorary Secretary to the Board of Management of the Hospital, Holman Kingdom, expressed his grateful appreciation of the public support given to this event and his sincere thanks to the performers for their donation.

Towards the end of January 1917 the local branch of the Girls' Friendly Society held an entertainment in the Parish Rooms in aid of the hospital. A religious play called a *"Mirror for Souls"* was performed and a good sum of money taken. According to a report in the *Chester Chronicle* for 11th August 1917, a series of functions were held during the weekend to augment the funds of the Auxiliary Hospital. On Saturday evening the local Subscription Band, assisted by artists from other bands, gave an open-air concert in Main Street, Frodsham. Unfortunately the details of the other events were not given.

A Midsummer Night's Dream

Later in August "The Close" School raised a further sum of over £44 - 00 with a performance of scenes from *"A Midsummer Night's Dream."* The managers used some of this money to purchase three special adjustable wheel chairs, six air cushions and six hot water bottles. Already in September 1915 it was reported that there had been comparatively few wounded soldiers coming in and therefore the expense of running the hospital was higher per head. Early in the following year greater numbers started to arrive and by December the total number of patients treated since March 1915 had reached 753.

More Operations

Despite the local community's generous support, in the autumn of 1917 the managers were finding it difficult to make ends meet. As Mr. J J Crosfield explained at the annual general meeting, the cost per patient per day was now more than 50 per cent greater than in the first year of the hospital. The reasons were twofold: firstly, everything bought by the hospital had become more expensive and, secondly, the very serious cases now being sent to Frodsham entailed great additional expense. Some idea of the extent of this problem can be seen from the fact that there were 37 operations carried out in May.

Mr. Crosfield went on to state that it was impossible to say what the cost would be in the future, but at least one shilling per head per day beyond the Army allowance would be needed. For an average of 120 men per day between £1000 and £1200 would be required during the next six months. Mr. Crosfield thought this was a large sum to find but, he said: *"I am confident everybody sympathises with our wounded Tommies and will wish to help them through the work we do in this, our local hospital."*

Finally he reminded his audience that subscriptions or donations would be most gratefully received by Mr. R H Dutton, Honorary Treasurer of the Board of Management at Parr's Bank, Main Street, Frodsham. Also that gifts in kind should be sent to the Matron at the hospital.

"Our Day"

Another example of voluntary effort - this time probably of only indirect benefit to the F.A.M.H. - is contained in a report in the Frodsham Parish Magazine for August 1918. On Saturday 10th August local volunteers organised a special event in the town called "Our Day" - to raise money to help the British Red Cross and the Order of St John to continue their work for wounded soldiers. Members of the public were urged to purchase and wear little Red Cross Flags. The organisers expressed their surprise that there were some people who did not seem to be aware of the *"splendid work done by these two Societies for our wounded soldiers."* To enlighten these people a special showing of the film *"From No Man's Land to Blighty"* had been arranged at the Picture Palace in Chapel Lane at 8pm on 9th August. The pictures would show how the wounded were brought in from the field, tended by doctors and nurses, and sent home in Red Cross trains.

The report goes on to state that the main event of "Our Day" will be a Fete at Mersey View Pleasure Grounds on 10th August from 2-30pm till 9pm. The entertainment will include sports, palmistry, tennis, competitions, Aunt Sally, music, dancing and tea, with the Frodsham Silver Band in attendance. The Marchioness of Cholmondeley had agreed to open the Fete and Lady Brooke will be present.

Unfortunately there is no mention in subsequent pages of how successful the event turned out to be and how much money was raised. But, undoubtedly, it was typical of the fund-raising ventures which enabled the Red Cross and the Order of St John to carry on with their important work.

J J Crosfield

From 1906 to 1915, Joseph John Crosfield, son of John Crosfield, along with his brother, George, ran the family firm of Crosfields Limited, soap manufacturers of Warrington. By 1914 they employed about 3000 people of whom 500 were women.

In 1892, the twenty six year old, Joseph Crosfield had married Alice Lilian, only daughter of Oliver Stokes Stack of Lansdown Crescent, London. Her father had been the District Superintendent of the Bengal Police. They were married at Christ Church, Paddington, and they decided to settle down in Frodsham. They lived at Netherdale, Carriage Drive, which is at the foot of Frodsham Hill.

Joseph was fond of cycling long distances - no doubt through Delamere Forest and on to Tarporley and Beeston - but his wife could not keep up, so he bought a tandem. But he soon discovered this meant he did most of the hard work so he invested in a BSA motorbike.

One of the few photographs of Mr. J J Crosfield - the Chairman of the Board of Management. He is sitting on the left of the Matron, Miss B Stevens, who is in the centre of the picture. On her right are Mr. Stanley Bower, Dr Selby, Sister Davis and Sister Mather.

They had two sons - Eric Owen born in 1893 and Guy Henry Goad born in 1897. After working in the family firm for many years, he became managing director in 1906. During these years he successfully resisted attempts by Lever Bros to take over Crosfields and maintained the continued growth of the company. In July 1915 he resigned his directorship after a dispute with the Board. During this period he had a number of local interests but early in the same year he had become Chairman of the Management Board of the Frodsham Auxiliary Military Hospital, which undertaking must have taken up a good deal of his time.

Like so many parents in the war Joseph Crosfield and his wife had to suffer the loss of their second son, Guy Henry, who was killed at the battle at Passchendaele in 1917. There is a memorial tablet to his memory in St Laurence Church, Frodsham.

After the war Mr. and Mrs. Crosfield moved south to Embley Park - Florence Nightingale's former home, near Romsey in Hampshire. During his retirement he served on various local committees and became High Sheriff of Southampton in 1932.

Joseph Crosfield was extremely generous to several charities. Among the gifts he made were £10,000 to Warrington Infirmary and £10,000 to King Edward's Hospital Fund. Without a doubt he must have contributed considerable sums to the hospital at Overton, whilst at the same time working hard and very ably as Chairman of the Board.

"Netherdale"- the house in Carriage Drive, Frodsham, built for Joseph Crosfield in 1892.

CHAPTER 5 -FROM THE BATTLEFIELD TO BLIGHTY
Transport and Care of the Wounded

Casualties were brought from the trenches in Northern France and Belgium to the coastal ports, where they were transferred to the south coast of England in hospital ships. Many of the wounded were taken to the Casualty Clearing Station at Eastleigh, near Southampton. From Eastleigh they were sent up by train to their various destinations, for example, Chester. At Chester Station they were met by ambulances or motorcars which transported them to the auxiliary hospitals in the area one of which was the Frodsham hospital.

The Casualty Clearing Station at Eastleigh had been established in April 1915. The purpose of this medical unit was to receive direct from the hospital ships the men who, in civil hospitals, would be classed as outpatients. These were the ones who were not too seriously wounded or ill, and therefore did not require special accommodation in ambulance trains. The casualties were sifted out at Eastleigh and sent to other hospitals by ordinary passenger trains or discharged as fit for duty after two or three weeks' stay in the Clearing Station. The following report appeared in the *Chester Chronicle* one day in May 1915: *"At 4-30 in the morning 52 more wounded soldiers arrived at Chester General Station in a hospital train. The "disembarkation" scenes have so often been described in our columns that we need only say that the men were carefully and expeditiously removed to the various hospitals. They were all tired and feeling the effects of their long journey."*

According to the report the numbers of men sent on to the various auxiliary hospitals were:

Richmond House 7
Hoole Bank 8
Frodsham 25
Vernon Institute, Saughall 6
Eaton Hall 5
Ledsham 4
Helsby 2
Bunbury 3
Ashton Hayes 2

The fact that a relatively large number of patients were despatched to Frodsham suggests that there were surplus beds at the Overton hospital in the spring as well as later in the year.

Another report in the *Chester Chronicle*, this time for May 8th 1915, gives more detail of how the men reached Frodsham and how they were treated upon arrival at Overton: *"They came from Southampton during the day, their train carrying over 300 wounded and sick soldiers. A number of Frodsham people lent their motorcars, and in these the 30 cases were conveyed to Frodsham. All the casualties were sitting up cases, and the ambulance was not required. The local ambulance men were present, however, and assisted in preparing the patients for their beds, under the superintendence of Doctors Ellison, Selby and Burton, and the hospital staff. By 8 o'clock all the soldiers were comfortably tucked up in bed, very thankful to have reached such homely quarters after continuous travelling practically since Wednesday."*

The reporter adds this interesting piece of information which confirms statements made earlier about the number of beds at Overton in the first few months: *"Eleven patients were still in, so the number of inmates now receiving attention is 41. The total accommodation being for 50 cases. The majority of the latest batch are suffering from bullet and shrapnel wounds, but none of them very serious."*

The fleet of ambulances parked near the hospital. Mr. Stanley Bower stands in the centre with Sergeant Bill Simmons on the right.

Reports of the wounded men arriving at Chester Station appear regularly in the local newspapers throughout the war years. One of the most graphic accounts was published in the *Chester Chronicle* on Saturday 8th July 1916. The train from Southampton steamed into Chester at 9 o'clock. The large crowd which had gathered at the station approaches cheered the wounded men as they were brought through to the waiting cars and ambulances. The reporter describes the scene as follows: *"Mud stained and torn tunics told how the men had come straight from the trenches. Crippled limbs and bandaged bodies showed their suffering. The walking wounded moved first and then the stretcher cases."*

In this instance Frodsham received 24 patients, including six cot cases.

The Patients

According to the official statistics, patients stayed at Overton for an average of 36.6 days - so it would appear that they were rehabilitated fairly quickly. Although from the photographs it is evident that a number of the men had amputated limbs, these operations almost certainly took place prior to their arrival at Frodsham. However there was a small operating theatre at the hospital and a certain amount of surgery was carried out there on a regular basis.

Joseph Brereton, whose family lived in Francis Row, Frodsham, served his time as a gas fitter. During the First World War he was sent to the hospital once a week, or at the time of an emergency, to ensure that the gas appliances - the water boiler etc - were in good working order during operations.

The evidence suggests that, though some of the patients were confined to bed for a while, many were in reasonable health and enjoying a period of convalescence.

The following report from the *Chester Chronicle* for June 1916 gives a rare glimpse of a typical scene at the Overton hospital:

"Our representative visited the hospital on Wednesday afternoon and found a number of the returned warriors enjoying the fresh air in the splendidly elevated grounds surrounding the hospital, and the view to be obtained was very different from the view which has met their eyes continually for the past few months! Inside, the hospital was most cheery, and visiting day helped to enliven the hours. A splendid array of flowers sent by the kindly disposed Frodsham people were artistically arranged in all parts of the commodious ward. Some of the soldiers were in bed, others - reading, some writing, others enjoying themselves in the recreation room."

The reporter goes on to heap praise on Frodsham people for their unstinting support for the hospital:

"The Frodsham people do not do things by halves, and in fitting up the hospital and lavishing gifts upon it day by day, they have been most thoughtful and generous. Two Chester men spoke highly of their treatment, and said it was quite a treat after all they had gone through. One of them described "the whole business" (i.e., the war) as nothing but murder on a large scale."

Cigarettes and Tobacco

One ironic feature of the provision for patients - in the light of modern medical knowledge - is the allowance of cigarettes. Since the hospital opened all the patients were provided with ten cigarettes a day, or the equivalent in smoking tobacco, and a box of matches. One wonders if smoking was allowed in the wards or if it was restricted to only certain places and certain times of day. A healthier pastime which patients enjoyed was the weekly shows provided by the Entertainment Committee. In 1917 the Committee had three members - Mrs. Hutchings, Mrs. Bury and Mrs. Glover and in December of that year they decided to hold a Sale to raise funds to help with the expense of running these shows. The event was to be held at Eversley, the home of Mr. and Mrs. Bury, on Wednesday 5th December at 2pm. Many people must have contributed generously as there were valuable items of needlework, china, glass and other antiques for sale. Unfortunately there is no record of how many people attended and how much money was raised.

Uniforms

All soldiers in military hospitals were required to wear the regulation dress supplied by the War Office. The patients at Overton wore a bright blue uniform with red collars and cuffs and white lapels. The standard footwear was brown boots. The other essential part of the uniform was a red tie, but the soldiers were allowed to wear their own regimental caps as can be seen below.

This photograph, dating from May 1917, shows a range of injuries to the patients. The beds have been carried out on to the cleared ground outside Ward III.

48

Maintaining Discipline

In addition to difficulties arising from the patients' medical needs, another set of problems facing the hospital authorities were those concerned with the upholding of discipline, especially among the convalescents. Although all the men would be still subject to military discipline, it would not be so easy to enforce in the more relaxed atmosphere of such an institution. From the few records which remain of the Overton Hospital, it is not easy to ascertain what the rules of daily living were but it must have been necessary, for example, for the able-bodied patients to observe certain times for meals, for medical treatment and for lights out at night. When the convalescent patients were allowed to leave the premises they would have to follow certain standards of behaviour and observe a curfew in the evening.

One of the few references to hospital discipline occurs in a report which appeared in the *Chester Chronicle* for Saturday 17th June 1916. A case had come before the local magistrates concerning a woman who lived in Ship Street, Frodsham. On a certain evening two soldiers from the Auxiliary Hospital were seen going into her house and, shortly afterwards, she went to purchase beer from the Red Lion.

She was charged with having procured beer for two soldiers who were undergoing treatment at the Frodsham Hospital. Mr. Stanley Bower, the Officer in Charge, said that practically the only breaches of discipline were caused through drink. The magistrate stated it was "cruel" of the woman to tempt the men in this way, as any misdemeanours committed by the soldiers under the influence of drink could result in severe military punishment. The magistrates decided that the woman should be fined 20s or serve 14 days imprisonment.

In the log book of the auxiliary hospital established in Ramsgate and staffed by Kent VAD, there are a number of references to patients being 'sent away', usually for drunkeness or failure to observe the curfew. In some instances, unruly patients were sent to nearby regular military hospitals where they would be subject to stricter discipline. Unfortunately there is no record any similar log book for the Overton Hospital, but it is reasonable to assume that these kind of problems arose there too, and that they were dealt with along the same lines.

Supplies to the Hospital

In most parts of the country basic food supplies were sent to auxiliary hospitals from county depots and, as far as we know, this is what happened in Frodsham. However, undoubtedly certain provisions, such as dairy products and fresh fruit, were obtained from the locality. One small example of this practice was foodstuffs purchased from the Berringtons. As a young woman, Mary Ann Berrington, became a cook at the hospital. Her parents kept a small-holding off Bellemonte Road with three or four cows, pigs and hens. During the war years soldiers were sent down regularly to collect eggs and milk for the hospital kitchens.

Soldiers from Overseas

Although the majority of the patients at Overton were serving with British regiments, a few were from distant parts of the British Empire. A number of Australian soldiers can be seen in the photographs - often recognisable by their distinctive caps - and men from Canada are also mentioned in the records. One other unique piece of evidence has come to light only recently - a small slab of sandstone showing the cleverly carved face of a soldier and round the edge is the inscription: **"OVERTON HOSP WOUNDED   1914 -18 AUSTRALIA."** (photograph below)Was this the only one of its kind ever made at the hospital or, at some stage, were there groups of men busy making sculptures in stone or wood not only as a record of their stay but also as a recreational activity?

A carving on sandstone of an Australian patient, probably a self-portrait.

On the right of the stove are Ptes Mundy and Harbar (with head bandaged), Nurse Cameron and the two Australian soldiers - Ptes Johnson and Rutledge. Sitting on the left are Ptes Evans, Smith and Fell, whilst Sgt Clarke, Sgt Gibbs and Pte Samson can be seen on the right.

Nurse Cameron, Sister Davis, Sister Mather, "Hughie" and Nurse Urmson with patients in Ward II, Christmas 1918.

Sister Mather in Ward II - Christmas 1917. The patients in the background are probably having a meal.

Maybe this is the same group of men having a meal who can seen in the photograph above. Judging by the amount of steam the food was piping hot! The men seated at the table are, left to right: Ptes Mundy, Evans, Pilling, Fell and Howgood.

Two Australian soldiers - Ptes Tranter and O'Rorke photographed near the main entrance.

Ptes Neyland, Harbar, Hopwood, Banks, Day, Nutting and Welsby outside Ward III in February 1918.

A group of patients outside the office building which in later years George Aitken converted into a private dwelling.

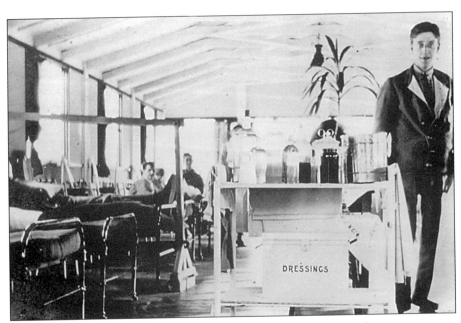

The medicine and dressings trolley. Note the frame for traction over the bed on the left.

In the centre at the rear is Pte Pycroft. The two men at the front are Pte Tommy Atkinson and Pte Hough.

Enjoying the summer - August 1917 - are Pte Spalding, Sgt Case, Ptes Rich, Tormey and Stevens along with, on the front row, Pte Saregan, Sgt Moor and Pte Barton.

A group of patients, including three bed cases, enjoying the fresh air outside Ward II in June 1917. The nature of many of their injuries is apparent from the photograph.

At the rear are Ptes Pickup and Rundle with, in the centre of the front row, Ptes Martin and Orr.

In the front row, left to right, are Ptes Lunsden, Bowler and Williams, with Sgt Moon sitting on the right. At the rear, left to right, are Ptes Saregan, Edmunds, Toomey, Buckle and Cormack, with Sister Davis in the middle of the group.

Nurse De Silva (on the right in the second row) and a colleague with a group of patients outside Ward III .

Nurse De Silva with another group of patients - probably in September 1917.

Nurses Dorothea Urmson (on the left) with two of her fellow nurses. It was Nurse Urmson who kept the album from which many of the photographs in this book are taken.

Nurses and patients in Fancy Dress - Christmas 1918. Such entertainments would play an important part in maintaining the morale of patients. Note Mr Stanley Bower and the Matron are sitting in the centre of the group.

CHAPTER 6 -THE STORIES OF A FEW INDIVIDUAL PATIENTS

The First Arrivals

In one of the first batches of wounded men to arrive at the Frodsham hospital was Corporal W H Youd whose family lived at the Bears Paw Hotel in Main Street. Corporal Youd had been attached to the Army Service Corps in France as a despatch rider. One day he suffered an injury to his foot and then, whilst on the ambulance wagon, he came under shell fire and received a nasty wound in his thigh. He arrived at the hospital early in June 1915 and, as far as we know, made a good recovery.

Another Frodsham man at the hospital in these early days was Arnold Lightfoot of the Guards who was wounded in November 1914. After receiving treatment in various hospitals he was sent home to recuperate. However his wound did not heal and so, after X-ray examination, the medical staff decided to remove pieces of bone from his hip. This was done and he made a slow recovery.

Australians at Overton

Miss Mary Gold tells the remarkable story of how two of her Australian relatives came to be patients at the hospital. An ancestor of hers, Samuel Moreton, emigrated to Melbourne in 1853. He had intended to take up farming but managed to set up in the more lucrative business of selling boots to gold diggers. A few years later he married and eventually he had five sons and two daughters. Three of the sons fought in the Gallipoli campaign. After a time at the battlefront, one was killed but the other two were wounded and sent to a military hospital in Manchester.

On hearing of their arrival, John Davies cycled to Manchester, found the boys and asked for them to be transferred to Frodsham where their relatives could visit them. The request was granted and they were duly moved to the hospital at Overton. The Davies family had a further connection with the hospital. For a time both mother and daughter served there as volunteer nurses. The photograph overleaf shows Mrs. Davies with her five sons and her daughter.

Sadly, Algernon died of his wounds on 27th October 1918 in West Flanders whilst in action with the Cheshire Regiment. The north porch of St Laurence's Church was restored in his memory in 1928. There is a plaque to this effect inside the porch.

The family of John Gifford Davies of Brook House, Main Street, Frodsham. Left to right: Don, Algernon, Elsie, Herbert, Colin and Bert with their mother, Edith Ellen sitting in the foreground.

Ambulance Driver

Another story of a former patient of the hospital was told by the late Mrs. Lyons of Bellemonte Road. Her father, Mr. Bill Simmons, of Bexhill-on-Sea, was serving with his regiment on the Western Front until the almost inevitable happened and he was wounded in battle. By chance he was sent to the hospital at Overton. When he had recovered sufficiently, he became an ambulance driver there. After the closure of the hospital in 1919 he decided to settle in Frodsham.

During this time the ambulances were kept at Overton Hall - the home of Mr. T Stanley Bower, who also provided facilities for the nurses at No. 95 Bellemonte Road. These premises not only provided some of the nurses with accommodation but also a rest place for them to use during their off-duty periods.

Pte Ellison

A Canadian visitor to Frodsham in the summer of 1999 related the story of how his father came to be a patient at the Overton hospital. Harry Ellison had joined the Cheshire Regiment in the early part of the war and "celebrated" his twenty first birthday on 19th June 1916 during the Battle of the Somme. Having survived that ordeal his regiment were in the thick of the fighting at

Passchendaele in 1917. One day, during an advance, he was moving slowly forward with five or six of his comrades when one of them suggested that they should stop for a bite to eat. They rested in an abandoned German bunker. Suddenly an enemy shell hit the roof above their heads. A large block of concrete came crashing down on top of him. In the turmoil and havoc of the battlefield he was left for dead. Miraculously he was found later by medical corps personnel who rescued him from No Man's Land.

His wounds were so extensive that in later life he could never recall where he was taken or what treatment he received. Finally he was brought by train to Chester and then by Red Cross ambulance to Overton. It fell to Dr Selby to inform his mother that her son was a patient at the hospital. Unfortunately little is known of his stay except that, because of his extensive wounds, he remained confined to bed.

One interesting detail has emerged, however, namely that the patients were visited on a regular basis by a group of ladies who encouraged the men to try some needlework. Over a period of months Harry Ellison learnt to stitch sufficiently well to produce a fine embroidery of his regimental badge.

Harry Ellison's embroidery of his regimental badge completed whilst convalescing at the Frodsham hospital.

After a few months at Overton, Private Ellison was transferred to another hospital in Maghull. In November 1918 he was finally discharged. Despite his lengthy treatment his health remained poor and Dr Selby advised him to escape from the cold, damp climate of England by emigrating. After finishing his time as an apprentice carpenter, he decided to follow his girlfriend to Canada. She had left with her parents a few years previously to join relatives in Winnipeg. Harry arrived in Canada in 1923 and married his fiancée in 1925.

Pte Harry Ellison (first on the left in the second row from the front) with some of his comrades in the Cheshire Regiment on the Western Front in 1916.

Pte Fred Lewis

Another intriguing story with a Canadian connection is that of Fred Lewis who became a patient at Overton during the First World War. Fred was born in London, the son of a Thames River worker. He had an unhappy childhood and emigrated to Canada with a friend and his family at the age of about 14 years. He worked until the war broke out and then joined the Canadian Army. After a while he was posted to France, where like so many others he was wounded. By chance he was sent to convalesce at the Frodsham hospital. During his stay he was invited to have tea with the Lawless family - the well known Frodsham bakers. There he was introduced to Elsie Lloyd who was in service with the family and through her he met Annie, her sister. This marked the start of their courtship.

After a time Fred went back to his regiment but continued to write to Annie. After the war he returned to Canada, found a job, bought a house and sent for Annie to join him. She sailed alone to Montreal and they married in London, Ontario, in 1920.

Pte Fred Lewis is seated in the second row from the front next to the soldier with his arm in a sling. Home from the "Push" almost certainly meant that these men had been injured during the Battle of the Somme in July 1916. The tents on the right are probably some of those which were issued by the Army but quickly sent back as surplus to requirements.

Sgt Major Finnerty

John Patrick Finnerty, whose family came from Ireland, was born in Birkenhead c. 1893. In 1912 he signed on as a regular soldier and eventually became a Sgt Major in the King's Horse Artillery. After the outbreak of war he fought on the Western Front for about two years before he was wounded. As a result of his injuries he lost two or three ribs. Also he had one of his fingers shot away. At the same time he began to suffer terribly from shell shock. After returning to England, he was sent to a military hospital in Shropshire and then to Frodsham for convalescence.

Whilst at Overton, Sgt Major Finnerty met his future wife. After a few weeks he became friendly with one of the nurses, Violet May Webb, and soon their romance blossomed. In 1919 they were married at St Laurence Church. They lived at 91 Main Street, Frodsham, and in due course they had a family of two children.

Pte Tindle

Pte John W Tindle served in the 4th Dorset Regiment. His service number was 23261. He was wounded on active service and spent some time recovering at Overton. In May 1918 he sent the photograph of himself shown below to the Matron and staff at the hospital. On the back he wrote the following message: *"In grateful remembrance of your kindness during my stay at the Frodsham Auxiliary Military Hospital. With best wishes, J W Tindle 29 May 1918."*

Pte Tindle

Lance Corporal Albert Worrall

Born in March 1899, Albert Worrall of Rake Lane, Helsby, enlisted on 12th April 1917. After training with the Manchesters, he transferred to the Notts and Derbyshire Regiment. Later in the year he was sent to the front line in Flanders. Towards the end of May 1918 a shell destroyed his section. He, and one other man, were the only survivors. Badly wounded in both legs, L/Cpl Worrall was taken prisoner by German troops.

Immediately German doctors operated on his legs. Much to his relief, the operation was successful and he began the slow and painful process of recovery. Conditions in the P.O.W. camp were grim and L/Cpl Worrall complained for years afterwards about the poor diet which he used to say did him more harm than the German shell.

Shortly after the Armistice of November 1918 he was given his release and eventually he arrived at the Frodsham Auxiliary Hospital where he continued his slow convalescence. One of the things upon which he often remarked in later life was how the "Thousand Steps" - between the Bellemonte Hotel and the top end of Overton village - presented him with quite a challenge on his crutches.

L/Cpl Worrall (on the left) with a comrade during his time at Overton hospital. Under their great coats, the hospital uniforms can just be seen.

War Graves

Most patients were nursed back to health but those who died were either buried in St Laurence's Churchyard, Frodsham, or at a cemetery in their home town. As far as we know all these soldiers were buried with full military honours. Of the ten War Graves in the Frodsham churchyard three men died at the Overton Hospital. They were: Pte Alfred Ernest Carter of the Leicestershire Regiment, whose funeral was described earlier; Pte Frederick George Price of the King's Shropshire Light Infantry who died on 2 August 1916 of wounds received in action. Finally, a Canadian soldier - Pte George McKay who died on 17 November 1918 age 24. His regimental details are given as 712371 78th Battalion, Canadian Infantry.

The grave of Pte McKay in the churchyard at Frodsham.

Pte Ridgeway and Corporal Taylor

In addition to the three deaths mentioned above, a few more patients died at the hospital, but they were buried elsewhere. Two soldiers in this category were Pte Ridgeway and Cpl Taylor. Pte Ridgeway of the 3rd London's died on Friday 9th November 1917. He had been at the hospital for six months suffering from wounds in the back which developed into septic poisoning. His home was in Manchester.

Cpl Taylor of the Royal Field Artillery died on 21st August 1917. He was 35 years old and he came from Southport. He was wounded in action on 7th August, tetanus set in and death resulted. His burial took place at Southport Cemetery.

CHAPTER 7 - CLOSURE AND THE AFTERMATH

A Tribute from Joseph Crosfield

The Frodsham Auxiliary Hospital closed in September 1919. In his statement accompanying the presentation of the final accounts in January 1920, Joseph Crosfield, the Chairman of the Board, explained that it had been kept open so long after the end of the war for the treatment of pensioners. As a result there had been no formal closing of the hospital and no opportunity to present the final accounts or to thank those who had served it so well, notably the Officer-in- Charge, the doctors, the Matron and the staff, the Hon. Treasurer and the Hon. Secretary.

Furthermore he went on to say that the accounts which he was now presenting did not show the true value of the contribution from the townspeople as the value of gifts other than money and the voluntary services rendered were not included. If these services were taken into account the total value of all contributions would far exceed £15000. As it was the total figure for donations stood at £7155 - 0s - 3d. (see the Statement of Accounts for March 1915 to September 1919 - Appendix I).

Mr. Crosfield added that since the hospital opened 3435 men had passed through it, and the total number of patient days i.e., the total number of days the men had spent in the hospital amounted to 156,292.

He concluded that the excellent work done by the hospital was shown not only by the accounts but also by the gratitude of the patients, and by the *"well merited decorations bestowed upon the Officer-in-Charge, the Matron and the various members of staff. Altogether it is a record on which Frodsham may look back with pride."*

Finally he added: *"It was a fine example of what can be accomplished by all working together for the common good."*

A Fine Memorial

In Chester Cathedral there is a special memorial to all the auxiliary hospitals in Cheshire in the First World War. On the wall of the Consistory Court is a beautifully made banner commemorating the voluntary work of the doctors, nurses and other staff who performed their duties faithfully during those difficult years. As the photograph shows, the banner depicts the badges of the St John's Ambulance Association and the British Red Cross on a background of the Tudor Rose, Scottish Thistle, Irish Shamrock and Welsh Leek. In the border is the Tree of Life and in its branches are the badges of all the regiments in which the sick and wounded soldiers served. The Arms of England,

Scotland, Wales and Ireland are shown in the four corners. At the top of the border are a silver dove and the rays of the Holy Spirit. The dove and the regimental badges were embroidered by disabled soldiers. On the back of the banner are the names of all the Voluntary Hospitals in Cheshire, including the Frodsham Auxiliary Hospital.

The banner (above) & plaque (opposite) in the Consistory Court, Chester Cathedral.

THE ST. JOHN AMBULANCE AND RED CROSS BANNER

THE BANNER commemorates the work of the Voluntary Hospitals in the County Palatine of Cheshire in the First World War, 1914-19. It was placed in the South Transept of the Cathedral in 1919. In 1964 it was cleaned and repaired by the Royal School of Needlework.

In the centre are the badges of the St. John Ambulance and the Red Cross. The background is a pattern of the Tudor Rose, Scottish Thistle, Irish Shamrock and Welsh Leek. In the border is the Tree of Life. In its branches are the badges of the Regiments, whose members were patients in the Voluntary Hospitals. At the four corners are the Arms of England, Scotland, Ireland and Wales. At the top of the border are a silver dove, the emblem of peace, and the rays of the Holy Spirit, shedding glory over the whole.

The Dove and the Regimental Badges were worked by disabled soldiers and sailors.

On the back of the Banner are the names of the Voluntary Hospitals, whose work it commemorates. They are as follows :

Abbeyfield, *Sandbach*
Abbotsford, *Rock Ferry*
Alderley Park, *Chelford*
Altrincham General Hospital
Ancoats Home, *Sandlebridge*
Ashton Hayes, *Chester*
Assembly Rooms, *Bowdon*
Barlow Fold, *Poynton*
Beech House, *Lymm*
Bolling, *Malpas*
Brabyns Hall, *Marple*
Bramhall & Cheadle
Hulme Auxiliary Hospital
Brookdale, *Alderley Edge*
Brookfield, *Lymm*
Brookfield, *Wilmslow*
Bromborough Auxiliary
Hospital
Brunner Mond Club,
Middlewich
Calveley Hall, *Tarporley*
Catsclough, *Winsford*
Cecil House, *Hale*
Cheadle House, *Cheadle*
Cheerbrook, *Nantwich*
Colshaw Hall, *Over Peover*
Cottage Hospital, *Runcorn*
Dowery, *Nantwich*
Frodsham Auxiliary Hospital
Haigh Lawn, *Altrincham*
Harewood, *Disley*

Heald Road, *Bowdon*
Heathfield, *Whitby Heath*
Heyesleigh, *Timperley*
Higgensfield, *Malpas*
Highfield Hall, *Bradbury*
Hilston House, *Altrincham*
Hoole Bank, *Chester*
Hoole House, *Chester*
Hurdsfield House, *Macclesfield*
Ingestre, *Ashton-on-Mersey*
John Leigh Hospital
Altrincham
Kilrie, *Knutsford*
Linden Lea, *Brooklands*
Manor Hill, *Birkenhead*
Moorfield, *Glossop*
Mottram Old Hall, *Mottram*
Neston Institute, *Neston*
New Bunnee, *Hoylake*
Nunsmere, *Sandiway*
Oakfields, *Upton*
Oaklands, *Preston Brook*
Parish Hall, *Acton*
Parkgate Hospital, *Parkgate*
Partington House, *Glossop*
Peckforton Castle, *Tarporley*
Pendlebury Memorial Hall,
Stockport
Penkett Road, *Wallasey*
Pickering Lodge, *Timperley*
Portal, *Tarporley*
Raddon Court, *Latchford*

Ravenscroft Hall, *Middlewich*
Raynor Croft, *Altrincham*
Recreation Hall, *Helsby*
Rock Bank, *Bollington*
Rode Hall, *Scholar Green*
Rose Hill, *Marple*
Somerford Park, *Congleton*
Stamford House,
Dunham Massey
St. John's Hospital, *Chester*
St. John's Hospital, *Dukinfield*
Stockton Heath, Auxiliary
Hospital
The Cenacle, *Wallasey*
The Chalet, *Hoylake*
The Ley, *Winnington*
Thelwall Heys, *Thelwall*
The Orchard, *Hale*
The Quinta, *Congleton*
The Rookery, *Tattenhall*
The Vicarage, *Runcorn*
Thornton Manor,
Thornton Hough
Vernon Institute, *Saughall*
Village Hall, *Tattenhall*
Village Hospital, *Bunbury*
Webb Orphanage, *Crewe*
Willington Hall, *Tarporley*
Wilton House, *Northwich*
Winsford Lodge, *Winsford*
Yew Tree Lane, *Northenden*

T Stanley Bower OBE

After the First World War Mr. Bower and Miss Stevens, the matron of Overton Hospital, opened a nursing home at Gambier Terrace - opposite the Anglican Cathedral in Liverpool.

As stated above, Mr. T Stanley Bower lived at Overton Hall, Five Crosses, Frodsham. He was the director of a Liverpool firm engaged in the coastal shipping business. After the war he became chairman of the Prince of Wales Hotel Company Ltd, Southport, and a director of the Overton Steamship Company.

He and his wife had one daughter, Elsa, who married Mr. Anthony Horner, whose father worked as an engineer for the Manchester Ship Canal Company. The young couple went out to Tanganyika - now Tanzania - where Mr. Horner worked as a dock construction engineer at Dar Es Salaam.

Stanley Bower had always had a keen interest in local affairs and during the 1920s he became President of the Frodsham Conservative Club and Chairman of the Frodsham Committee of the Eddisbury Divisional Conservative Association. A founder member of the Frodsham and District Agricultural and Horticultural Society, he served as its chairman for many years. Also he had become a prominent freemason and was a member of several lodges.

According to the writer of his obituary in the *Chester Chronicle* he was *"a generous supporter of all the local churches and chapels. No one appealed in vain for his support to any deserving cause."*

In the early 1930s he helped to establish a centre for the unemployed at Castle Park. Perhaps his greatest achievement was during the war when, as we have seen, he was chiefly instrumental in inaugurating the F.A.M.H.

To quote again from his obituary: *"it was through his leadership and beneficence that it became recognised as one of best equipped medical institutions of its kind in the country."*

For four and a half years he served as the Officer-in-Charge there and it was in recognition of these services that in 1919 Mr. Bower was awarded the OBE. He died in 1935 aged seventy and was buried at Southport Cemetery.

Overton Hall, Five Crosses, Frodsham - formerly the home of Mr. T Stanley Bower OBE.

No.95 Bellemonte Road, Frodsham, the house at which Mr. Bower provided rest and recreation facilities for the nurses in their off-duty periods.

The managers gave one of the these silver bookmarks to every member of staff shortly after the hospital closed in September 1919.

Some of the houses built on the hospital site as they appear today in 2001.

Four generations of the family who played a major part in the development of the Mersey View and the Bellemonte Recreation Grounds. On the right is Mrs. Parker Hoose, next to her is her daughter, Mrs. Annie Bate. On her right is Mrs. Zillah Sampson with her daughter, Juliet. This photograph was taken on 17th October 1923 at the wedding of George Aitken and Millicent Bate, and shows their bungalow in the background - the building formerly used as office premises in the days of the hospital.

The Fate of the Buildings

After it closed down as an Auxiliary Military Hospital in September 1919 the premises never reverted to their former use - as a roller skating rink. During the 1920s concerts and dances, including Carnival Balls, were frequently held in the main hall but in the late 1930s it ceased to be used for entertainment. At the same time Mr. George Aitken made use of some of the buildings. He converted the former office premises, which stood in front of the entrance to the main hall, into a dwelling and from that time on it was generally known as George Aitken's bungalow. The building which had the glass-panelled doors (Ward III) became his garage where he kept a couple of wagons and a charabanc. In the 1930s he ran regular charabanc trips to Liverpool and North Wales.

During the Second World War the hall was requisitioned by the government and it became a depot for the Ministry of Food.

The Maple Floor

Some years ago the late Mrs. Beb Savage told the following remarkable story:

"A few years after the war representatives of an American company visiting Frodsham were so impressed with the quality of this sprung maple floor that they decided to buy a large part of it. After carefully numbering each piece it was taken up and sent to Pennsylvania where it was re-laid in a Pittsburgh ten-pin bowling alley. By coincidence my brother-in-law lived in Pittsburgh and when I was visiting him some years later someone mentioned this connection with Frodsham. When the owners were told, I was invited to view the floor and walk on 'a little bit of Frodsham' in the U.S.A."

Mrs. Savage said how thrilled she had been to see it and to read a small plaque on the wall which stated that this fine maple floor came from a former military hospital in Frodsham, England.

In the 1960s the former hospital premises were used by the late Mr. Alan Oultram for his heating-oil business but eventually the firm moved to a more convenient site. In 1984 the remaining buildings were demolished to make way for private houses.

In Conclusion

Although there were those who said that Bellemonte was an inconvenient location for a hospital, the site on the slopes of Overton Hill must have been in many ways idyllic, especially in summer time. For the thousands of soldiers returning from the Somme, Mons, Ypres and the other battlefields of Northern France and Belgium, the rural tranquillity of Overton provided a wonderful rehabilitation centre.

As we have seen it became a sizeable establishment and it served its intended purpose extremely well. Certainly the 3435 patients who recovered their health at Overton were glad of the treatment they received there. Many, if not all, went away with fond memories of Frodsham Auxiliary Hospital.

Bibliography

British Red Cross - Accounts for Auxiliary Hospitals 1918

British Red Cross - Cheshire Branch Report and Accounts for the Year 1919.

Cynthia O'Neill - *"A Picture of Health - Hospitals and Nursing in Old Picture Postcards"* - Meadow Books 1991

Major-General Sir W G Macpherson - *"Medical Services General History"* Volume I 1919

Vera Brittain - *"Testament of Youth"* - Virago Press 1978

Thekla Bowker - *"The Story of British VAD Work in the Great War"* Melrose, London c. 1918

F W Longbottom - *"Chester in the Great War"* 1920

George D Mealor - *"An Unorthodox History of Oaklands"* 1923

Paul Creswick et al. - *"Kent's Care for the Wounded"* Hodder & Stoughton 1915

Frodsham Parish Magazines 1915 - 1919

Chester Chronicle 1915 - 1919

Runcorn Weekly News 1915 - 1919

Hazel Basford - Quex Park Auxiliary Military Hospital 1914 - 1919

Log Book of Ramsgate Auxiliary Hospital - Imperial War Museum - Miscellaneous 2018

Appendices

Appendix 1

Frodsham Auxiliary Military Hospital
Statement of Accounts to 31 December 1916

Receipts	£ - s - d
Subscriptions	2141 - 18 - 2
Maintenance of beds	425 - 9 - 4
Concerts	98 - 8 - 0
Workmen's Contribution	393 - 15 - 4
Miscellaneous	163 - 18 - 6
Capitation Grant	6068 - 7 - 0
	9291 - 16 - 4

Payments	£ - s - d
Equipment, inc. adaptations of original ward & construction of new one	2303 - 10 - 5
Maintenance of building & repairs	517 - 15 - 7
Fuel, Light & Water	432 - 0 - 8
Petty Cash Payments	60 - 0 - 0
Insurance of buildings & Nurses National Insurance Stamps	36 - 4 - 7
Chemists, Dressings, Drugs, Medicine, Surgical Appliances	604 - 5 - 11
Salaries, Wages & Nurses' Home	932 - 15 - 2
Provisions	3393 - 0 - 11
Laundries	574 - 10 - 2
Printing, Advertising & Stationery	36 - 13 - 6
Postage & Travelling Expenses	57 - 13 - 5
Newspapers	9 - 0 - 11
Rates & Taxes	9 - 12 - 3
Repairs & Furniture	2 - 14 - 9
Rent	18 - 15 - 0
X-Ray Treatment	12 - 2 - 0
Massage	23 - 5 - 0
Miscellaneous	51 - 7 - 8
Balance in hand	216 - 8 - 5
	9291 - 16 - 4

Statement of Accounts for Five Months ending May 31 1917

Receipts	£	s	d
Balance in hand Jan 1 1917	216 -	8 -	5
Donations	243 -	17 -	9
Army Allowance	1727 -	17 -	0
Farmers' Red Cross Fund (£420-13-7)			
& sundry subs	497 -	14 -	4
Debit balance	134 -	15 -	2
	2820 -	12 -	8

Payments	£	s	d
Maintenance			
Provisions	1350 -	14 -	10
Surgery & Dispensary	290 -	1 -	9
Domestic	457 -	16 -	4
Establishment	75 -	0 -	9
Salaries, Wages, etc	315-	19 -	1
Miscellaneous	40 -	1 -	2
Administration			
Management	11 -	4 -	4
Finance Rent, Rates & Taxes	56 -	15-	11
Building & Equipment			
Land & Building	200 -	0 -	0
Equipment	22 -	18 -	6
	2820 -	12 -	8

Statement of Accounts from the Opening of the Hospital March 1915 to the Closing Date, September, 1919.

Receipts

	£	s	d
Donations, etc	7155	0	3
Capitation Grants	25091	8	0
	32246	8	3
Deficit	2	7	2
	32248	15	5

Expenditure

	£	s	d
Maintenance			
Provisions	15945	2	8
Surgery & Dispensary	1972	11	7
Domestic	5675	11	4
Establishment	1470	2	0
Salaries, Wages, etc	3925	0	8
Miscellaneous	381	0	10
	29369	9	1

Administration						
Management	11	4	4			
Finance	2	0	10			
				13	5	2
Rent, Rates, Taxes, etc				71	9	3
Building and Equipment				2794	11	11
				32248	15	5

(Signed) R.H.DUTTON, Hon. Treasurer.

Appendix II

WAR GRAVES - St Laurence Parish Church, Frodsham

Reference: CRO P8 2619/9/6

1/Leicesters 7614 Private A Carter d. 18/12/1915 E(left)46

RFA 96911 A/Bdr E Lazenby died 30/12/1915 NE 6 1 7

KSLI 19722 Private FG Price died 2/8/1916 E left 2 1

RDC 25717 Private C Percival died 9/1/1917 E R 3 3

Cheshires 446 Sgt W Worrall died 9/5/1917 N E 4 10

RN HMS "Canada" Smn L Ellams died 23/4/1918 NE 3 7

Cheshires 77248 Private A Hopley died 14/7/1918 N E 3 12

Bn Canadians 712371 Private G McKay d. 17/11/1918 E L 4 3

Cheshires 35080 Private W Massey 25/11/1918 NE 2 2

MGC* 64863 Corporal J Bostock died 9/2/1919 NE 2 10

*(MGC - Machine Gun Corps)

Appendix III

Other Local Voluntary Hospitals

The nearest auxiliary hospitals to Frodsham were established at Helsby {see page 22}, Preston Brook and Runcorn. At Preston Brook Lord Daresbury made available his Victorian mansion, Oaklands, and, with the help of the local Red Cross, he organised a hospital there. The Oaklands was situated where the Daresbury Park Hotel now stands. In 1918 the hospital had thirty beds and the patients average residence was 69 days.

Hospitals in Runcorn

During the war 3460 servicemen were treated at the Cottage Hospital and at the Parish Church Vicarage Voluntary Hospital, Highlands Road, Runcorn. Canon Howard Perrin established and ran the latter institution. After the war he was awarded the OBE for his unfailing endeavours on behalf of the sick and wounded soldiers who were looked after there.

Auxiliary Hospitals in Kent

In Kent most of the towns and larger villages set up their own Voluntary Aid Detachments in the years immediately prior to the First World War. The main purpose of these units was to organise auxiliary hospitals and then to provide the staff to man them. In order to prepare themselves for these duties VAD members attended lectures and engaged in practical work. Sometimes they gained valuable experience by working at a civil or military hospital in the locality.

These units received help and encouragement from their parent body - the British Red Cross or the St John's Ambulance Association. After the outbreak of war auxiliary hospitals were established in a variety of buildings - parish halls, schools, private houses, disused hotels and even, in one case, at a yacht club. In nearly all instances local residents contributed liberally in money and equipment.

Typical of many small hospitals set up in Kent is the following:

"KENT 20, TENTERDEN, was started in the town by Mrs Peel at the request of Lady Cranbrook in 1911. The members of the detachment, at first under Dr Skinner as Commandant, have continuously been preparing themselves for any emergency. When mobilised in October 1914 the detachment sent reliefs to a local hospital until November, when a Red Cross Hospital was opened with sixteen beds. This was furnished to a great extent by the local residents, who were also most generous sending contributions. On November 30th 1914, the first party of Belgian soldiers, fifteen in number, arrived."

{ page 116 *"Kent's Care of the Wounded"* by Paul Creswick and others.}

Also Published by Avid Publications

THETIS - THE ADMIRALTY REGRETS –THE DISASTER IN LIVERPOOL BAY

The definitive minute by minute account of this terrible tragedy in 1939 when 99 men lost their lives as HM Submarine *Thetis* undertook her first and only dive. With new photographs and documents as well as a new foreword by Derek Arnold, a survivors son, and a new postscript by maritime historian David Roberts. Why didn't anyone cut open the submarine? Why was there no urgency in the Admiralty's rescue system? Did the Admiralty really regret? by C.Warren & J.Benson

ISBN 0 9521020 8 0   £9.50 + £1.50 p&p

HMS THETIS – SECRETS AND SCANDAL – AFTERMATH OF A DISASTER.

by David Roberts

The sinking of *Thetis* cost 99 men their lives and is still today the worst submarine disaster in British History. This latest book contains interviews with relatives of victims; sons, daughters, brothers, sisters and those very rare ladies, living widows. Also here are never before seen documents from the time; Offers of outside help, Secret Navy reports and even descriptions of bodies for identification. Why did the Official Inquiry blame nobody, explaining it away as 'an unfortunate sequence of events'? Why did the civil action on behalf of the widow's fail? Did the Admiralty cover it up? How much did Churchill know? How were those left behind treated? A huge publicly subscribed disaster fund was collected for the relatives. How was this managed and distributed? Who got what and why? What ever happened to the money that was left?

'a book that shocks...tells the hidden story of those left behind'   - Sea Breezes.

' now known as the Hillsborough of its day... a disaster surrounded by injustice' - Liverpool Echo

ISBN 0 9521020 0 5   £8.99 + £1.50 p&p

LUSITANIA - UPDATED MERSEYSIDE EDITION by Colin Simpson

THE definitive work on the real story surrounding this still mysterious ship.

On the 7th of May 1915 the Cunard vessel Lusitania was torpedoed by a German submarine off the Old Head of Kinsale on the south west coast of Ireland resulting in the loss of the vessel itself and 1,201 men, women and children. It also ultimately resulted in the United States entry to the First World War. More than eighty five years on the story of the *Lusitania* continues to be shrouded in mystery and suspicion. What was her real cargo? Why wasn't she protected? Why did she sink so quickly? Containing rare photographs from Germany and elsewhere; it is a truly intriguing and fascinating tale.

ISBN 0 95201020 6 4   £9.50 + £1.50 p&p

CAMMELL LAIRD - THE GOLDEN YEARS by David Roberts.

Foreword by Frank Field MP

Looks back at the world famous shipyard's history with particular focus upon the 1960s and 70s when Lairds were engaged in the building of Polaris Nuclear submarines. A unique look at the history of this yard that contains many photographs and references.

'Captures life in the prosperous years of the historic Birkenhead shipyard'- Liverpool Echo

'Puts into perspective...the strikes...the Polaris contract...and those who worked at the yard'- Sea Breezes

ISBN 09521020 2 1   £5.99 + £0.80 p&p

LIFE AT LAIRDS - MEMORIES OF WORKING SHIPYARD MEN
by David Roberts

When Cammell Lairds has gone and we are a generation or two down the line who will answer the questions 'What did they do there?' 'What was it like?' This book answers the questions. - Sea Breezes

A Piece of Social History – Liverpool Echo

Life at Lairds is a book of more than 120 pages about what life was like for the thousands of ordinary people that worked in the world famous Birkenhead shipyard. Contains many rare photographs of Lairds, its' ships and its' surroundings.

ISBN 0 9521020 1 3 £6.99 + £1.50 p&p

FASTER THAN THE WIND - A HISTORY GUIDE TO THE LIVERPOOL TO HOLYHEAD TELEGRAPH.
by Frank Large

Take a journey along the one of most spectacular coastlines in Britain, the beautiful hills and countryside of North Wales and Wirral. On a clear day it is possible to see just how signals were sent along the coast to and from Liverpool. This book contains full details of the intriguing and little known sites of the substantial remains of the Liverpool to Holyhead Telegraph Stations. A second journey can then be taken into the fascinating workings of such a telegraph and those people involved in creating and using the signalling system and what life was really like living and working at the telegraph stations more than 100 years ago.

ISBN 0 9521020 9 9 £8.95 + £1.50 p&p

IRON CLIPPER – 'TAYLEUR' – THE WHITE STAR LINE'S 'FIRST TITANIC'
by H.F. Starkey

'Iron Clipper' is subtitled 'The First Titanic' for it tells the story of the first White Star liner to be lost on her maiden voyage. Built on the Upper Mersey at Warrington, the *'Tayleur'* tragedy of 1854 and the *'Titanic'* catastrophe of 1912 are disasters which have so much in common that the many coincidences make this factual book appear to be a work which is stranger than fiction.

ISBN 1 902964 00 4 £7.50+ £1.40 p&p

SCHOONER PORT - TWO CENTURIES OF UPPER MERSEY SAIL
by H.F. Starkey

Schooner Port tells the story of the part Runcorn and navigation of the upper Mersey played in the Industrial Revolution and of the contribution of merchants, the shipbuilders, and the crews in making Britain 'The Workshop of the World'. Also recounted is something of the courage and tragedy, which was the lot of many flatmen and seamen who helped build British industry on the strength of the shipping fleet.

'Recognised as the only authoritative work on this particular subject '- Sea Breezes

'Packed with hard facts and illustrated with some rare old photographs, this rare book should command a wide readership'. - Liverpool Echo

ISBN 0 9521020 5 6 £8.95 + £1.50 p&p

THE GOLDEN WRECK - THE TRAGEDY OF THE ROYAL CHARTER
by Alexander McKee

The effects great of the great hurricane of October 1859 were to shock the nation. 133 ships were sunk, 90 were badly damaged and almost 800 people lost their lives.

More than half of those that perished were on one ship - The *Royal Charter.*

The *Royal Charter* has a special place in maritime history as one of the greatest ever peacetime disasters. She was built at Sandycroft on the River Dee, the next-door neighbour to the river that was to become her home...the River Mersey. Soon after she was launched...sideways because of her great size for the day, she perhaps seemed ill starred in that whilst being towed down the river she grounded upon a sandbank off Flint, North Wales, and suffered serious damage to her main keel.

She eventually completed her maiden voyage to Melbourne in record time and her owners were able to boast about their new service 'England to Australia in under 60 days'.

Just a few short years later she was returning home and was hours away from disembarking her charges in Liverpool... until, when rounding Anglesey on the northern coast of Wales...disaster struck in the form of a Force 12 hurricane.

The people of the small village of Moelfre, Anglesey, came to the aid of the vessel and those from the ship who tried to escape the lashing waves and the deadly rocks. News of the wreck soon spread and the *Royal Charter's* other cargo, gold, became the focus of people's attention. Was all of it ever recovered? If not where did it go? The *Royal Charter's* gold still has the power to attract the adventurous and this book also explores attempts at salvage and treasure hunting more than 140 years on.

ISBN 1 9029640 2 0   £9.50 & 1.50 p&p

ALL at SEA - Memories of Maritime Merseyside
Compiled by Ev Draper. Foreword by Radio Merseyside's Linda McDermott
Introduction by David Roberts - Maritime Historian

A new book in conjunction with BBC Radio Merseyside's programme of the same name brings the voices of Merseyside seafarers and their lives to the printed page. Here are the stories of brave men, now pensioners, who survived horrendous incidents in the last two wars; stories of luxury liners, from Captains to cabin crew, of young lads forging their identity cards to get away to sea, and of their first eye-opening voyages.

ALL at SEA brings back the sounds and the smells of the docks, which remain vivid in so many people's minds, of busy tugs up and down the river, of men lost at sea; of women serving their country in different ways, and of those who provided guiding lights home. But through all the stories, there's one shining thread, the pride of Merseysiders in their seagoing traditions.

If you want real stories of the sea, told from the heart, by real people about real times and places, then this is a book for you.

ISBN 1 902964 12 8   £5.99 + £1.25 p&p

FORGOTTEN EMPRESS - THE TRAGEDY OF THE *EMPRESS OF IRELAND*
- by David Zeni

Tells the fascinating story of the Canadian Pacific Passenger liner *RMS Empress of Ireland*. On her way home to Liverpool from Canada, she was sunk in a collision on the St. Lawrence River. Two years after the *Titanic,* it was, in terms of passenger fatalities, an even greater tragedy. These two ships, along with the *Lusitania,* form a triumvirate of maritime tragedies, all within a three year period, that sent shock waves around the world.

Yet whilst *Titanic* and *Lusitania* seem to be almost household names, the disaster that befell the *Empress of Ireland* has until now always been shrouded in the cloak of history, as impenetrable as the fog that brought about her total loss, along with 1,012 lives, on 29th May 1914. With a chilling connection to the 'Crippen Murders' and containing never-before-published material, *Forgotten Empress* grips the reader in such a way it is hard to put aside... a thoroughly excellent book.

...dubbed 'The 'Forgotten Empress'...the second in a shocking trio of tragedies at sea...sandwiched in between the disasters of the Titanic *and the* Lusitania, *...it was a sudden death... that sent Liverpool into mourning...'* Liverpool Echo

' Zeni brings a fresh, moment by moment urgency to this real life tragic drama' Winnipeg Free Press

ISBN 1 902964 15 2 £10.50 + £2.00 p&p

LUSITANIA AND BEYOND - THE STORY OF CAPTAIN WILLIAM THOMAS TURNER
by Mitch Peeke & Kevin Walsh- Johnson. Illustrated by John Gray

There are many accounts of the great maritime disasters, but very few portraits of the people at the centre of these vast, tragic events. William Thomas Turner was captain of the RMS *Lusitania* when the giant liner was sunk by a German submarine attack in May 1915, with the loss of more than 1,200 passengers and crew. Turner survived, and this is his story.

A Merseyside man, he came from Victorian seafaring stock and his sole ambition was always to go to sea. Turner became the outstanding seaman of his time, who had learned his craft the hard way- by experience.

The loss of the *Lusitania*, bound for Liverpool from New York, shattered his world and over the years he has been accused of treachery, stubbornness, ignorance and much worse. This book gives the true, remarkable story of Captain William Thomas Turner, the last Master of the doomed *Lusitania.*

'...the Admiralty made 'thoroughly discreditable attempts to blame Turner for the loss'... 'clears Captain Turner's name once and for all'... Liverpool Echo

ISBN 0 902964 14 4 £7.99 + £1.25 p&p

A WELCOME IN THE HILLSIDES?
- The Merseyside and North Wales Experience of Evacuation 1939-1945
by Jill Wallis

A book that is both informative and moving, brilliantly researched, with the stories of the thousands of children who left the dangers of Merseyside for the safety of North Wales during World War II.

ISBN 1 902964 13 6 £9.95 + £1.90 p&p

JUST NUISANCE AB - His full story
by Terence Sisson

The amazing but true story of the only dog that was officially enlisted into British Royal Navy, a Great Dane whose name was Nuisance, his official rank and name was AB Just Nuisance. Famed for his preference for the company of navy ratings (he wasn't too keen on Officers) in and around the famous World War II naval base of Simonstown, South Africa, Nuisance helped many a sailor rejoin his ship after a night on the town.

Today his own statue overlooking the bay off the Cape of Good Hope commemorates AB Just Nuisance.

£7.50 + £1.20 p&p

VIDEOS

Cammell Laird - Old Ships and Hardships - the story of a shipyard.

After an extensive search for moving footage of this world famous shipyard at work a video of the history of this shipyard has at last been compiled. How Cammell Laird served the nation through two World Wars, building world famous vessels like the *Rodney, Hood, Mauritania, Ark Royal, Windsor Castle* and many more, up to the tragic day in 1993 when Lairds was shut down.

The story of the yard is also told through the voices of the men who worked at Lairds; Welders, cranedrivers, electricians and plumbers, they tell of the hardships of building ships in all weathers and the lighter moments that came from some of the 'characters' of the yard.

'All in a Day's work.' Volumes I & II
– a look at working lives on the River Mersey.

Just when you might have thought that the River Mersey was dead and buried the biggest surprise of all comes along. There is life in the old dog yet! The River Mersey is alive and well. Liverpool, Birkenhead, Tranmere, Eastham and Runcorn are still places that enjoy marine traffic and employ people working on the river. There are interviews with River Pilots, shipbuilders, shiprepairers, tugmen and dredgermen that show that the age-old crafts and seamanship itself are still as strong as they ever were. There is also archive footage of working life on the river.

Features Rock Boats, Mersey Ferries, the Bunker boats & crews on the Mersey, the Vessel Tracking System for river traffic, new vessels on the river, lockmasters and much more.

All videos are priced at £14.99 including post and packaging in UK.

Videos are also available in international formats price £17.99 + P&P £3.50.